Contents

Cats, dogs, and fleas

What do cats eat
for breakfast?

Mice Crispies.

What did the cat call the
mice on rollerblades?

Meals on wheels.

6

What is a kitten's favourite colour?

Purr-ple.

What do you call it when a kitten stops?

A paws.

What kind of dog
likes to take a bath?

A shampoodle.

What is a dog's
favourite dessert?

Pup-cakes.

What city do dogs like to visit?

New Yorkie.

Where should you never take your dog?

A flea market!

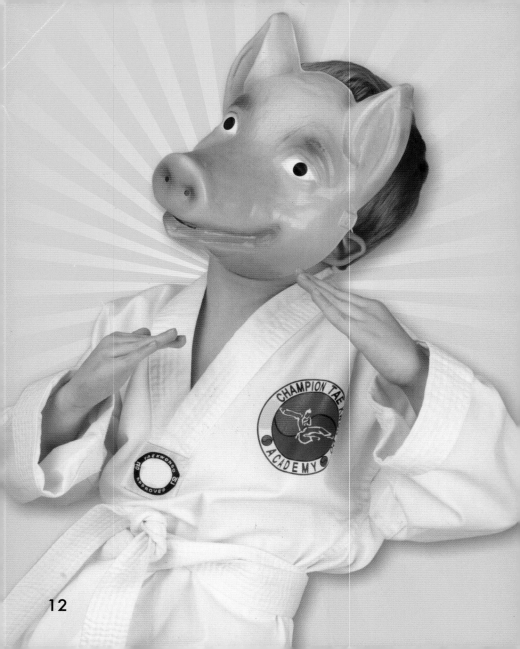

12

What do you call a pig that knows tae kwon do?

A pork chop.

What do you get when you cross a pig and a cactus?

A porky-pine.

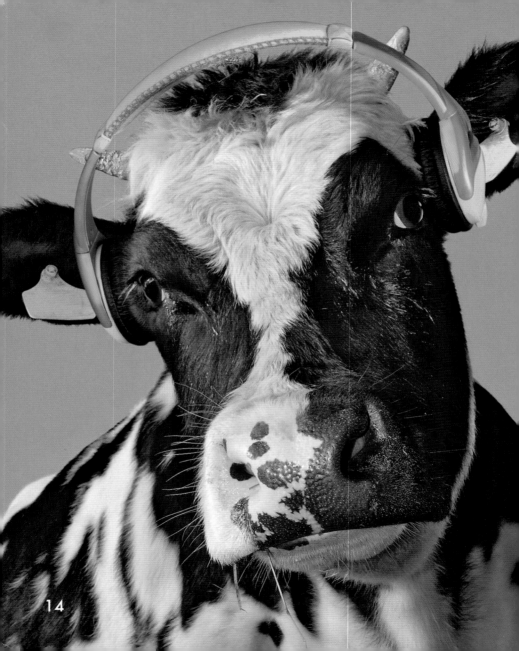

What is a cow's favourite subject at school?

Moo-sic.

What does a cow do on a Friday night?

It watches a moo-vie.

What is a rabbit's favourite dance?

Hip-Hop.

Why was the rabbit crying?

He was unhoppy.

What do you give
a sick bird?

A tweetment.

What do you get when
you cross a caterpillar
with a parrot?

A walkie-talkie.

What do you call
a fish that doesn't
have an eye?

Fsh.

What do you get when you
cross a shark and a cow?

**I don't know, but you
wouldn't want to milk it!**

What do ducks like
to eat with soup?
Quackers.

What time of the day
does a duck wake up?
At the quack of dawn.

Further reading

Humphrey's Ha-Ha-Ha Joke Book, Betty B. Birney (Faber Children's Books, 2011)

The Giggle-a-Day Joke Book, (Child of Achievement Awards) (HarperCollins, 2011)

Create your own joke

Follow these steps to write your own joke:

1. Pick a topic. A one-word noun is good. For example, "cat".

2. Make a list of words connected to your topic - "claws", "tail", "wool", "fur", "kitten", and words that rhyme with those words and your topic - "snores", "snail", "bitten", "mitten", "hat", "rat".

3. Make a list of joke types. For example: "What happened when ..." "What's the difference between ..."

4. Try out different jokes, fitting your words from step 2 into the joke types from step 3. For example, "What happened when the cat ate a ball of wool?" "It had mittens!"